BECOMING

PHENOMENAL

EVERY WOMAN'S GUIDE TO DEVELOPING UNMATCHED CONFIDENCE

Volume 1

CHIGAEMEZU REGINA

BECOMING PHENOMENAL
Every Woman's Guide To Developing Unmatched Confidence
Volume 1

Copyright © 2021 by Chigaemezu Regina
Reviews: *olua.regina@gmail.com*
Facebook: *Chigaemezu Regina Richard*
Instagram: *Chigaemezu_Regina*

ISBN: 978-978-58024-1-2

Published by:
Gamechangers Media
Abuja, Nigeria
Tel: +234 806 599 0019

FOREWORD

Because it is now somewhat increasingly difficult to clearly get what people mean when they call themselves feminists, given how much of a 'war of the sexes' it has become in some quarters, I like to always prefix my feminist identity with *classical*. As in, I'm a classical feminist – my way of saying I'm [only] all in for the original idea of feminism that is both commonsensical and just, the clamour for equal access to opportunities for both men and women. Really, it just doesn't make sense to, in qualitative terms, draw comparisons between men and women to the effect that men are *better*. And whether you draw your inspiration from religious arguments or cultural sentiments is, to me, absolutely immaterial.

By the way, my feminist conviction is barely 8 years younger than me. I only grew up to find that there was already a name for an opinion I formed when I was about eight. It was at a performance in church at the time, and a bunch of kids had come on stage to render a song in the class of what was called *Special Number*:

I woke up in the morning

I looked round the whole world

And wondered what it could be

Without a woman (2x)

God didn't make a mistake at all! 2x

For making me a woman

As an 8-year-old living with my mum and an older and a younger sister, who all saw to it that I lacked nothing, and whose soul was yet to be tainted by *chauvinism*, it just made sense to me that there is something priceless about being a woman. And, by extension, there is something mischievous about any man who thinks less of women. Frankly, just as nothing feels as safe as a mother's bosom to any child, even so do we all feel about the women in our respective lives.

There is something particularly thrilling about this book. It's author. Spending all four of my university years in the same class with her, and having kept in touch for, currently, six years afterwards, and being a huge fan of the fantastic work she's been doing in the women capacity building space for the last couple of years, I can only confess that there couldn't have been a better person to take on this conversation. Being a woman of substance herself, ravishingly beautiful in body and really rich in heart and mind, Regina represents everything we celebrate in womanhood. We can only hope for a world where more women get to choose to thread this path less travelled, the path of influence and significance.

It is somewhat disturbing to stomach the opinion (boldly aired by Regina) that *womanhood is chaotic*, an idea that essentially captures the concern around women's world appearing to be a divided house, evident in the so much bickering and backstabbing that many women continue to suffer in the hands of other women. True, these vices are characteristically human, and as such common to both sexes, but the damning reports countless women continue to put out there, all pointing to women's hostility to women, beats the imagination. It is sad that many women think that something is wrong with every other woman. It is disturbing that many women prefer male company because they dread female company, making frantic effort to keep their private affairs from other women for fear of sabotage. It beats the imagination how easily some women water down the accomplishments of other women, how they bad-mouth other women's appearances, brazenly talk down their ideas and fiercely attack their opinions.

Interestingly, this book ingeniously points to what may appear to be the reason for this chaos, the fact that insecurities and unrealized potentials could literally incite envy in anyone, and the truth that a lack of confidence can keep people small enough to keep picking quarrels with people who dare greatness. Coming from centuries of relegation and deprivation, women who have not been able to break the jinx of patriarchy nor smash the glass ceilings of corporate life struggle to stomach the fact that some others have done so for themselves. Coming from ages of shaming and oppression, women who have not been able to overcome the pressure to stay in shape, metaphorically, find it difficult to applaud those who have gone on to take their destiny in their own hands, living life on their own terms.

Regina thinks, and I really agree, that developing unmatched confidence is the panacea to this perennial chaos and rivalry that characterize womanhood. No doubt, it takes a measure of confidence for one to realize that the sky is too extended for two birds to collide, that collaboration trumps competition every time, that forging a common front against the injustices being meted out against women in society is the surest path to realizing the long-and-hard-fought-for gender equality, that women who are doing well in various climes should serve as inspiration to others and never as a threat to anyone. To say the least, there simply is enough greatness to go round. And women can help one another level up.

This book equally stands out in the way it outlines practical steps that could see one renegotiate one's confidence level, while at the same time shedding light on the factors that are responsible for low confidence levels. As such, it is expected that this book passes for a handbook on unlocking one's potentials and unleashing one's genius. And I can't think of anyone who could have done a better job than Regina has already done in here.

Whatever you do, endeavour to read this book. And rest assured of a 101% return on investment of money and time; you can take my word to the bank.

Cornelius Ndubuisi
Author, *The Wonder of Books* & *Thinking Differently*

CONTENT

REALITY CHECK!

It is commonplace to find women being comfortable with having multiple male folks not just as friends but as "besties," who are sometimes preferred to their female counterpart. Anyone would naturally wonder why, as the usual assumption is that females would easily mingle and bond intimately with their kind. But no, many women now prefer guys as their close buddies, not their fellow ladies anymore.

Some women now seem to find worthy allies in the other gender, and see other women as competitors and traitors. The question is, what's it with all the fuss women have among themselves? Why the fight? The envy? The jealousy? Backstabbing? Comparison and the mistrust? Why so much mischief? Can this be attributed to nature? Perhaps nature may have created women to be enemies of one another; there are common everyday examples of female classmates, roommates, and co-workers who are like two rivers that never meet. Or is this a result of nurture? Could it be that the environment contributed to the chaos in women's world? Why is there so much anger and controversy in the camp of women?

I would have never thought that two organisms of the same species would rather choose an organism from another species over theirs. I mean, even animals don't do this. So why us? I could go on and on asking questions just to reach an understanding of the basis of this issue because it's something I can't seem to wrap my head around.

Moving away from the unending questions, we are faced with an even more challenging question: How possible, and how soon can women evolve to the level of becoming aware of their respective individuality, strength and power, and fully become active in nation-building if they still engage in this intra-gender war?

I call it an "intra-gender war" because it is within the camp of women. If the camp is in disarray, how can the clamour for equal opportunities with the male gender become a reality? Would this ever happen, or is it going to end as a mirage? These questions and more have been my concern lately as a woman who's been actively pursuing a path in women development.

On this journey, I've had a lot of surprises. I have experienced things that made me wonder if any of the rancour and bickering among the female folks is worth it. And one thing I can say is that, until women resolve the invisible enemy that cripples their *Becoming*, as against the historic and patriarchal stereotypes which for long has limited women, they will continue to dance to the tune the society dictates without showing much progress. This is the bitter truth, and we must swallow it if we truly want to make progress. Women must now emerge. We have to unbox our differences and potentials, and resolve to engender progress within our camp.

What is even more disheartening to know is that a lot of women on this journey called life are yet to realize the essence of womanhood. What is the essence of womanhood? BECOMING! Now, the basic questions are: Who are you *Becoming*? What are you *Becoming*? How are you *Becoming*?

Society has erroneously taught us that the crux of our journey as women ends in *Becoming* a "wife" or "home manager,"—which is not entirely wrong. And as women, we have for long gladly accepted this narrative to be the totality of womanhood, without batting an eyelid. Not only have we accepted it, we have also successfully passed this notion down from generation to generation. As it is, this trend would continue many years down the line if we, as women, don't aggressively address it.

Women are no second-hand creatures! Actually, it takes more to be a woman. A woman is a "womb-man" on an assignment to incubate, birth, and nurture greatness as ideas, wealth, relationship, influence, impact, and, most importantly, life. If you've ever tried doing any of these, you would know for certain that it requires more than just a swing of your hands.

The journey to *Becoming* any or all of these is overwhelming, and not without difficulties. As a woman, you are more than just a *creature*; you are a *creator*, an artefact, and a raw material for creating many other things. You are more! You see, there's a lot a woman can offer as a nurturer, a multiplier, a manager, a caregiver, and a caretaker.

And to interpret the effect of a woman's *Becoming* is to show what is more important: finding a balance in her unique abilities and possibilities. It is this sense of balance that makes a woman phenomenal. And yes, the level of balance a woman possesses in managing these roles, and even more, shows an awareness of herself, personal strength, and ministry, which is in finding clarity of purpose, and deliberately living it out.

I cannot overemphasize the importance of purpose discovery for a woman. It may have been carelessly thrown around for a long time, but discovering one's self is the secret to living a more productive and fulfilling life. A woman who lives life outside purpose is like a hen that abandons her chick and makes them vulnerable to the hawk.

Life without purpose will inevitably end in abuse and misuse—which is the reason most women just live lives dutifully to fulfill the charge of "increase and multiply" in a reproductive-child bearing context without being bothered about increasing or multiplying the other deposits of ideas, influence, and resources in them. It is the lack of foresight that incapacitates and blinds her to her purpose, which consists in filling her other gaps as a solution finder and problem-solver for societal relevance.

Is *Become Phenomenal* realizable? The answer is YES! There are women who exhibit a high level of skill in the way they manage their numerous responsibilities—self, family, friends, marriage, business, career—and still thrive; the likes of Ody Adede Agbor, Wendy Ologe, Dr. Ngozi Okonjo-Iweala, and a host of others, even unmarried. I call these women PHENOMENALS because of their mastery of balance in their career, business, and their dedication to upholding family values. These women have discovered their strengths and gained clarity of their life's purpose and assignment. Hence, they live each day of their lives concentrated and focused on what truly matters.

One simple truth to be shared here is this, *Becoming Phenomenal* does not promise to be a walk in the park. It requires a lot of effort, time, commitment, and focus. You must come prepared to follow the process, and learn as you go along the way.

To live an outstanding life, one of impact, you need work on yourself, realizing that tomorrow will only yield the harvest of the seed you sow today.

This book, **Becoming Phenomenal**, is a piece for every woman who desires to be more and do more. It promises to sharpen women's awareness, discovery, and development, while addressing the challenges of womanhood, thus helping every woman rewrite narratives against her existence, live her best life, and become the best version of herself.

In this First Volume, I have shared ideas and strategies to help you identify and deconstruct limiting beliefs while developing unmatched confidence, which is the sustaining principle to staying phenomenal, making impact, influence and income. I challenge you not only to do whatever it takes to read this book in its entirety, but to use what you learn on a daily. It is the application of what you learn that is necessary to your *becoming phenomenal*.

CHAPTER ONE

WOMANHOOD IS CHAOTIC

"The only person you are destined to become is the person you decide to be."

~ Ralph Waldo Emerson

* * *

G rowing up in a small town in Eastern Nigeria, there were things we considered tradition because they were the norm for us as kids. We looked forward to weekends because there was hardly any weekend that came by without a celebration: the birth of a child, an anniversary, a birthday, a child's naming ceremony, a programme in church, an activity at school, you just name it. There just had to be something to celebrate each weekend. And so we eagerly looked forward to them. Besides the food and fun activities at the party, the girls also enjoyed showing up in what they thought were their best wears.

However, it was not just about dressing up and looking good; it was more about looking better than every other girl at the party—talk about the "slay queen" life. There was just this sense of pride that came with being recognized as the best dressed, even if no one actually gets to say it. Everyone just knew. We wanted the other girls to desire our style and dress sense, and, of course, the other girls wanted us to do the same.

Reminiscing on this experience, I can clearly recall how the adults who were around us—especially mothers and aunties—significantly influenced and fanned this competitive tendency in us. Somehow, they made us see friends as rivals and imposters, and with each appearance, party, church, any gathering at all, it only got worse. Actually, it appeared as if they were the ones vying for a trophy for best dressed daughter because they would invest so much of their time and energy into making each outshine the other girls. Was this a bad thing? Probably not. I mean, who wouldn't want to look good when going out to a function?

The fundamental problem was that they were unintentionally planting seeds of discord, enmity, and unhealthy competition into our heads as young girls. Parties were just one thing. We were unconsciously influenced to compete not just in the way we dressed but in the way we spoke, walked, related with people, even down to our classroom performance and almost everything we set out to do as girls. To us, everyone was a rival: neighbours, classmates, schoolmates, age mates, etc.

Lately, through my research as a girl-child advocate and one who mentors young adult women, I have come to understand that the same ignorant upbringing of the girl child by the significant adults in their lives forms the basis of how these girls eventually get to perceive one another as they grow up.

To be honest, ignorant upbringing shapes all our lives, whether you are female or not, but growing up to meet these same things outside places us in a state of conformity. Can you now clearly see the genesis of the chaos in womanhood, the reason we never agree but compete and backstab? It shows how childhood experiences either makes or mars a woman's ideology and journey to *Becoming.*

Once anyone has been submerged in a particular belief for too long, they become it. The idea most times is to make the child appear more reserved, homely, well-trained and, most importantly, marriageable. Environmental and motherly nurturing has, overtime, predisposed women to treachery, bickering and jealousy. And the implication is that women, in their different disadvantaged (cultural or patriarchal) societal spheres and with chaotic nurture, have been recreated into becoming rivals and competitors, instead of empowering and complementing one another to discover their individual strengths and voices.

Even more sadly and annoying is how a woman shames a fellow woman for their misfortunes. Without carrying out a survey, one can see that cultural practices like female genital mutilation, uncivilized widowhood practices, the shame and stigma associated with barrenness, body shaming and name calling and its likes, are mostly championed and supported by women. You hardly see a man take a blade to circumcise a girl, or see a group of men force a woman to drink all sorts of unhealthy things in the name of honouring the dead. It is also not very common to hear or see a man body shaming a woman. It is still the women in the community who chair these practices and enforce them to the letter. If any woman tries to defy their "constitution," they tag her all sorts of derogatory names and shame her to no end. And guess who does the shaming and name calling the most? Women! Or have you not observed this trend? You would ordinarily expect that a woman should be able to empathize with her fellow woman and understand why she wouldn't or shouldn't have to go through certain practices. But no, they would rather instigate the entire sisterhood against the one who is different.

So, who bells the cat from this somewhat unconscious effort of rivalry amongst women?

It is you, the WOMAN!

During my secondary school days, I loved and wished to attend a Unity School, or at least one of the model schools in town. Why? Because everyone I knew had gone to those schools. It wasn't because they were the best schools at the time, but because the environment and the relative bickering amongst our significant adults made the schools appear rosy. My late mother objected to the idea on the ground that life there was more about competition than studies proper. She wasn't necessarily afraid of competition in the literary sense, but she knew the outcome such an exposure would have on me in the long run, which is the basis for the perennial chaos amongst women.

She thought I should go to what others take to be the least school in the neighborhood, where she believed I will shine my light as brightly as the star that I am. This was also the case for all my sister-siblings. Why? My late mum knew the seed from which rivalry grows and did all she could to nip it in the bud. Did she succeed? Yes! At least I can boldly say I do not see what another owns and envy it, maliciously wishing it were mine. I rarely get jealous or envious of people's achievements. If you have known me for a long time, you will attest to my sweetness as a friend.

I can vividly recall how my late mother never fell for those antics. She would always remind my sisters and I that we are all the best of our kind. There was no favorite, and there was no one better than the other. To even make matters plain, she gave each of us a special name, a name that depicted our strengths, and never cowered us on our weaknesses. Although she didn't have the best of education, she clearly understood the power of words and how to use it on each of us without bruising the ego of another.

Here's one thing I learned from my late mother, and which I have grown to know as the reason I am less likely a contributor to this womanhood chaos: the woman is the major deciding factor for the temperament in a home. And I am not just saying this because I am a woman. If you study many homes closely—or better still, inspect yours—you'd realize that in most cases, children take up personalities, attitudes and character traits from the whims and inclinations of their mother. This is definitely not an attempt to dismiss the role of a man in a child's upbringing but to simply establish an undisputable fact: a woman plays a major role in what becomes of a child. However, it is this inherent quest to make the most of their homes that lure some women to resort to unseen and unintended rivalry against one another.

And so, as women, to quit the unseen rivalry and bickering amongst us, we must reposition phenomenally, re-evaluate our dispositions towards one another, unbundle our limiting lenses and develop unmatched confidence to journey the path to becoming phenomenal.

CHAPTER TWO

REPOSITIONING PHENOMENALLY

*"This is YOUR book. With it, comes the responsibility
to be a better woman…"*

~ Michael Reid

* * *

It's no longer news that many women in this part of the world grew up with some self/culture limiting beliefs that have stayed with them year in, year out. One of these beliefs is the idea that a woman's sole mission in life is to grow up, get married, and become a housewife, attending to both her husband and children's needs. And anyone who tried to challenge this long entrenched belief was met with strong resistance, for which many had to succumb for peace to reign. They reasoned, "If getting married and losing all my dreams meant peace, then so be it!" With this, they resigned to fate.

This mentality is the main reason the gist of self-discovery for women seems difficult to internalize or apply. For many years, we've been subtly indoctrinated with this notion by even those we look up to, especially the significant adults who raised and mentored us. Breaking away from it now feels like a struggle that we are most likely not prepared for. We were taught and, you could say, convinced that greatness, purpose, and all the amazing things of life are the exclusive preserve of the male gender. I use the word "convinced" because while we were restricted from doing the things we wanted, we watched the male in our lives do these things and succeed at them. It only cemented the idea that such things were designed just for them – and not for us. So, we "conveniently" ignored our passion, trivialized our purpose and career leanings, and made them into ladders with which the male folks climb to the peak of their career and attain success in their respective fields of endeavour. As far as we were concerned, it was their responsibility to cater for our so many needs, for which we could only sit by the sidelines and watch them thrive.

Dear woman, success or greatness is not gender-sensitive. In recent times, opportunities and privileges are rather becoming gender blind. Factors that limited our becoming great are gradually been smashed by new beliefs and approaches to doing things.

To say the least, greatness has stopped discriminating against women, as every day women all over the world are shattering glass ceilings, breaking boundaries, and setting new records in various industries. By shattering ceilings, I don't mean earning the right to vote and be voted for, or merely being able to sit in spaces which were once reserved for men. Of course, we've gone past those. We have gone way beyond just the regular, and all of those achievements are glaring. Women are now breaking old records and setting new ones. Platforms are being created and opportunities being made available through policies and global movements for women to thrive. But the truth is, only a prepared woman who has developed enough breadth of capacity will lay hold of these opportunities. Like it is said, success is what happens when opportunity meets preparation. So, it is only the woman who prepares and decides to reposition, those who have been living purpose and intentionally working to make positive impact in their immediate society that will really thrive – while those who are not deliberate about developing their potentials and honing their skills will continue to watch in admiration.

It's the dawn of repositioning! And we have just a few women pushing to rewrite the old narrative, as a greater number of women still see themselves as the light of their parlour, salt of their kitchen and sugar in the bedroom. Everything about their mindset is confined to just building their homes without a balance on the other areas of life.

Wake up, woman! If you must come on this journey, then you must set yourself up in freedom. You must work to be independent. With independence comes choices and alternatives. The world is adjusting to seeing the humanness in women. The world is ready to embrace your uniqueness and see you bloom – phenomenally!

I believe in the mad shift happening for women. I believe in the awakening, the consciousness, the awareness of a today's woman who's eager to thrive and succeed. I believe in her vision to break the barriers against her existence, to evolve and get involved; and no longer to stand by the corridors to watch things happen.

For two years into the social development sector as a gender development expert, coach and women capacity builder, I have been working and raising my voice towards achieving a more women-enabled society through my organization, Dare Women for Change Initiative, by helping other women realize the power in their voices, uplevel their mindset and skills to be equipped for the new economy, one day, per time. Women are now beginning to redefine the way they see themselves and their fellow women who are out to achieve real and intentional success. YES. We are repositioning phenomenally.

It is a decade of future-forward women. The ongoing awakening and awareness is for women to brace up, develop coping skills and build the capacity necessary to get involved. It is no longer business as before, as the narrative is changing.

Wake up, woman!

You must rediscover your strength and stretch your ability and capabilities. I used the word "rediscover" because the world has emerged and only women who reposition to become phenomenal will thrive. Repositioning is both intentional and distinctive. It is the decision to uncover your inner strengths, develop your personal powers, and commit to action in order to grow, personally. It is the decision to move from desiring to evolve to actually working out strategies to do so. It is the decision to develop interest and learn the new economy skills. Repositioning is a process, and must first start with your desire to be more by actually doing more.

Wake up, woman, and reposition. It is the awakened, repositioned woman, the one who realizes her value, identifies her life's purpose, and positioned to live purposefully, I have called a **Phenomenal**. The Phenomenal woman is a one who is aware of the strength of her voice, has identified her purpose, and is unapologetically pursuing it, as she pursues other life callings. She is a woman who understands that it takes synergy to rise. By synergy, I mean the collaboration and support of others, especially her kind, as it will take more than one person to rise in the different sectors; she needs other women change agents and solution finders. The strategy and process will require that women support their fellow women, collaborate and complement one another, and work together to re-negotiate their place in society. And this must be done very intentionally.

The phenomenal lady is the new generational woman. She is ready to question stereotypes and trump all odds to become the best version of herself. She is one who is no longer held back by fear nor live in the anxiety of what others think of her existence. She is not bothered by the labels society has tagged to her humanness. She is a visionary, strong-willed, resilient and ambitious. She's a balanced woman, one who has through many experiences and processes mastered how to creatively live an epic life and remarkably leave the imprints of impact to her name.

The phenomenal woman is an intelligent and smart woman, who strives to discover who she is and has the courage to live it out. She sets goals in line with her purpose and works towards achieving these goals. She is focused and not distracted by flimsy shiny toys. She works to build financial independence.

She has intellectual foresight to build upon her career, chairs in boardrooms, and can be seen in the corridors of influence. Her ability to command attention in business and marketplaces, while making smart decisions that stand out, marks her out as outstanding.

The phenomenal woman discusses ideas and not people. And knows the net worth of networking aright, hence she grows her circle with likeminded people who discuss intentional strategies, processes and systems of growth that can birth the results and success they seek. Intelligence is the new sexy!

The phenomenal woman is a complete package. She is purpose-driven and result-oriented. She attracts with her brain, not only her body. She understands clearly that her worth is not in the fullness of her breasts but in the power of her brain. Her sense elevates her beyond sex and makes her a force to reckon with. Just like Chimamanda Adichie, Kamala Harris, Ngozi Okonjo-Iweala,

Amanda Gorman, Wangari Mathai, Malala, Ibukun Awosika, Tara Durutoye, and a host of other great women, the world celebrates at the mention of their names, not because of how curvy, full, sexy or dress down they look, but because the impact in their different sectors stands them out. If you don't know these names, be kind to search them out and study them. Great role models they are.

The phenomenal woman is the kind that inspires other women unto greatness. She beams light for others to see and leads the way for others to follow.

A phenomenal woman is what T.D Jakes describes as a "table marked, *RESERVED*." She is an exhibit marked, "Look but do not touch." Not only that, she is the envy of the ordinary, and a connoisseur with the mighty. Her words are far more glamorous than her clothes. She is not the faddish, foolish, fanatical icon of the day. She is as timeless as a concerto in C minor. Now, that's some bragging rights gained from TD Jakes description of the kind of woman called *Phenomenal*.

The phenomenal woman is a woman who has learnt to wear her crown well. She's learnt just how to sit on the throne that has her name on it. Learnt to appreciate the gift God put into her by appreciating her strength.

The phenomenal woman is a solution finder. Where people see problems, she sees opportunity and bears solutions. This is because she has an abundance mindset. The phenomenal woman is a selfless woman. She moves beyond what Brian Tracy calls WIIFM (What Is In It For Me) to what I have called WCIG (What Can I Give). The question, what can I give, depicts selflessness. As a woman with an abundance mindset, she looks to solve problems and not complain about or compound them.

The phenomenal woman is principled and disciplined in words and action. She is not a loud and lousy talker; she chooses her words carefully. She knows better when to open her mouth to share her opinion and when to keep silent.

The phenomenal woman is YOU! Yes, YOU. She's a voice. She's light. And she's love.

CHAPTER THREE

TOWARDS BECOMING PHENOMENAL

"You cannot dream yourself into a character; you must hammer and forge yourself one."

~ Henry David Thoreau

* * *

Society has normalized the question, "What do you want to become in life?" instead of, "Who are you Becoming?" I have found out through my work with women that the former question informs the mindset and reason women struggle to find their voice and often end up dependent.

The question, "What do you want to become?" implies a certain destination to one's life and requires a definite, closed answer. The question narrows one's visions, dreams, aspirations, and ambition. Hence, limits women from the very beginning, even as society further places cultural limitations on her.

I recall my teenage years, when all dreamt about was to become a lawyer. Once anybody asked, "What do you want to become in life?" I didn't think twice before echoing: lawyer! Why? Society sold me the mindset that one has to be one thing to be valuable. And of the things, if you are not a doctor, an engineer or an accountant, you are nothing. Gifts, talents, and other skills were neglected. Even to say that one wants to become a teacher sounded annoying. The significant adults in our lives programmed that thinking, hence limiting once tendency to express innate gifts, talents and skills.

However, to rewrite this narrative is to normalize asking: *who are you Becoming*? This question implies a journey and process that involves the individual's decision to grow, discover herself, and manifest her better version, while becoming her best.

The question, who are you *becoming*, caters to growth; the experiences and encounters of a woman and her reactions to them determine who she's *becoming*. This goes to show you that *becoming* is an ongoing process, more than it is a destination. It is in the byproduct as much as it is in the end result. It is not a quick-fix drive-through; it is a sustained follow-through. *Becoming Phenomenal* is about upgrading to the best version of oneself in one's different endeavors; it is simply about progress and growth – and not how perfect one grows.

As a process, *becoming* is a journey, and only the living travels this path. *Becoming Phenomenal* is the intentional act of shifting from one condition or situation to another. It is not left to chance or accident. It is not a hopeful event. It is you steadily on the journey to becoming better tomorrow than you were yesterday and are today.

So, journeying the path to becoming phenomenal is to believe in your ability, and be able to balance the different hats of womanhood: mother, wife, home manager, teacher, baker, cook, chef, student, professional, and anything and everything you dream of. It equally entails the understanding that every stage and phase of your life requires you to learn a lesson that will prepare you for the next phase.

Let me share a personal experience with you.

I used to be that person who would make excuses for anything called responsibility. Growing up, I was raised in church. Although not a preacher's kid, my late mother ensured we participated in most church activities, especially in children and youth programmes. I found it disturbing at the time, but later got to appreciating all the effort my mother was making as I grew past each stage and age of my life. Being involved in all those activities as a child opened me up to a lot of learning. Aside from arming myself with the word of God, I grew in the revelation of who God is, knew him for myself, and grew in confidence, or so I thought.

When I moved to high school, the values I had learned from home and church informed my actions, regulated my behaviour, and cultured my reactions to life and my fellow students.

Reading this, you must be imagining an overtly confident person. Sorry to burst your bubble, sweetheart, I wasn't. I struggled to show up. Not because I lacked the ability to, but because the shy side of me took reign over my life.

This is one thing I have observed mentoring young girls in high School. There is this feeling of inadequacy that engulfs them, and if not properly addressed, grows with them into becoming shy adults.

So, in high school I was that girl who knew she had a lot to offer but yet a shadow of herself. As a golden fish has no hiding place, I was still fished out by my school administration to serve as the head girl in high school. Even in my feeling of inadequacy and shyness, I was still sought after as the best to pilot the studentship.

Did I do well? Yes. I had an amazing year as the head girl. But I still struggled. I had the imposter syndrome, the feeling that you are actually not the awesome fellow people perceive you to be. And so, I struggled with low self-esteem.

The only thing that really got me active was if a task's deadline was seconds away and was practically knocking on my door. Only then would I go into overdrive with efforts to commit to responsibility and complete the said task.

Between 2009 and 2013, my university years, things changed. I met this friend on campus, a course mate, who has over the years, 10 years and counting now, continued to demonstrate his belief in my abilities by always sending me materials to read, sharing courses I could take to improve, and even educational movies to watch. All these was in a bid to change my mindset and motivate me to take action. He genuinely always wanted me to dare and be more. But this was entirely challenging for me because I kept on struggling to believe in my own abilities or trust the words of friends like him who never ceased to mention how creative and brilliant I am, the power I possess, and the grace I carry.

It wasn't until 2019 that I began to believe in my abilities and see what others have been seeing in me all along. Before 2019, I always embarrassed myself and my ancestors as a result of my lack of commitment, intentionality, and, most importantly, lack of confidence to undergo the process of becoming my best.

Although I was quite easy going, the girl who smiled and cheered a lot, I was scared of having people in my personal space. This made me lose opportunities, quality friendships and connections, and made very little impact in the lives of others, for almost two decades. Today, the story is altogether different. I am no longer the shy, noncommittal girl. I have become my definition of a phenomenal woman, a lady who dares to be distinctively different.

Today, I thrive in confidence. I am recognized as a woman development expert, one in the number of women who are championing the mad shift happening for women to believe in themselves, develop confidence, and harness the great potential in them.

I hear you ask, "What changed?" I will tell you. I had a mind shift and uncovered my personal power. To uncover my personal power, I had to build on my strengths and people-relationship, I learned to work with like-minds, embraced mentorship, and had a role model I looked up to. I learned from experiences that didn't break me but strengthened me and made me and wiser. You could be in my shoes even now. I understand this is the plight of so many women. If this is you or not exactly your case to the extreme, you have no worries.

In this volume, I have shared exactly how I got out of that seemingly never-ending cycle of lack of self-confidence into my journey to becoming a phenomenal woman and living a purposeful and fulfilling life.

And since I changed my mindset and decided to be intentional about staying confident, I have never remained the same!

Before I show you the limiting signposts, I realized from my personal experience and work with women, that everything about *becoming phenomenal* rises and falls on personal responsibility. It is crucial, therefore, to emphasize that you are solely responsible for what you become: phenomenal, epic, failure, outstanding, you name it. For instance, the decision to read through the sheets of this book, pick your lessons, and run with it to become a better you, is entirely up to you.

What you have in your hands is partly the story of my *becoming*, the lessons and experiences that have birthed all you see and admire in me. And I have no doubt it will also push you to kick start or continue on your journey to *becoming phenomenal* while developing unmatched confidence to sustain your grace.

THE PROCESS OF BECOMING PHENOMENAL

There is a result-orientated, tested and trusted, process any woman on the journey to becoming worthy, valuable and virtuous should undergo. From my study of great women, I have identified the three components of this process, constituting the pathway to becoming phenomenal: The Self-Knowledge Process, the Systematic Process, and the Social Knowledge.

THE SELF-KNOWLEDGE PROCESS

For you to be of any true value, phenomenally, there's got to be total mastery of yourself, your vision, ```purpose, strength and your weaknesses.

A shocking truth I discovered is that you don't need fluency or eloquence to become confident. This is part of the lies we have believed, a deceit that has burdened many of us and even buried some of us inside the goldmine that is us. Listen, you don't need intellectuality and experience to become confident in your Who, What and Why.

You just need to discover yourself. What you really need is the knowledge of your truth. The truth of who you are. It is knowledge that gives clarity, and clarity breeds confidence. Let me simply tell you that all the things outside that you are chasing after in order to feel powerful and confident won't cut it. Confidence must come from the inside – not from external things. It must flow from the realization of who you are, what you are worth, and the things you can achieve.

Knowledge of the self can be found and established only within you. It is generated from within and not outside of you. It is you channeling your strengths and unveiling the things already deposited in you. It is this revelation that switched things for me, and today I have grown to become a voice for women development, championing the mad shift happening for women. What you have in your hands is the story of my becoming, the lessons and experiences that have birthed all people see and admire about me.

Self-knowledge is the bedrock to becoming phenomenal. It is the consciousness and awareness you have about who you are. Remember, becoming phenomenal is a journey and a process, hence you are knowledgeable about your daily existence. Self-knowledge is what you have discovered about you by yourself. It is not what the significant adults in your life told you about you. It is your discovery about yourself. And how do you become knowledgeable about yourself? There are two key questions to help you achieve that.

First question: Who am I? It was Socrates, the ancient Greek philosopher, who said an unexamined life is not worth living. So the question, "Who are you?" bothers on identity and mindset.

Second question: Who am I becoming? This is about understanding your vision and assignment or purpose in life. Becoming phenomenal is about living a life of purpose and a life of service. Hence, in the pathway or process of self-knowledge, you get to understand who you are and actualize your purpose.

Mindset: Your mindset is the first concern to address when it comes to realizing the goal of becoming phenomenal. Your mindset is your mental disposition towards things that happen in your life. The mind is like a battlefield with sets of activities and experiences fighting to gain access and rule over your life. To stay knowledgeable about your identity and your journey to becoming phenomenal, you just have to learn to guard your mind. And to guard the mind is to be in charge of gateways of your life—the eyes, the mouth and the ears. What are you constantly feeding your eyes, ears and mouth? Remember, as a man thinketh in his heart, so is he. If you keep saying how inadequate you are, your mind processes only your inadequacies and you keep struggling. If you keep looking down on yourself in your vision, that's what your mind interprets, and that is what you will become. If you keep hearing negatives, your mind will only keep interpreting negatives. Jettison your limiting beliefs!

Mindset Scenario:

Lady A lost her job in the peak of the pandemic, and because her gateways are constantly feed with positives, she sees opportunities, listens to soul lifting inspirations and affirms positivity to herself on a daily basis. She reacts to losing her job joyfully as she is fully aware of her strengths and optimistic to securing a new job, soonest.

Lady B loses her job, but because she has constantly fed herself with negative news on the media of how jobs are difficult in the pandemic and how companies are laying off staff regardless of their years of experience, she begins to panic about what life holds for her and is pessimistic to receiving any news or opportunity that sounds true.

Are you Lady A or B? Lady A has the growth mindset, the mindset that sees positivity, whereas Lady B has the fixed mindset, the thinking that things always remain the same and cannot change. So, which of these ladies do you think will become outstanding and achieve greatness moving forward? Your guess is as good as mine.

A phenomenal woman's mindset is the mindset of growth. Becoming phenomenal is about *being* before it is about *doing*. *Being* is about your nature, while *doing* is activity. Be phenomenal; be renewed by the transformation of your mind.

Identity: Your identity reflects your mind. What you call yourself is who you become. I am **Chigaemezu Regina**. I grew to know this as my name, but going through the experiences of life, I have realized that my name is not my identity. My identity is who I am becoming, and who I am becoming depends on the clarity I have of my life's assignment.

It is not in the title as married woman, graduate, doctor, or other such titles. It is in my assignment, my calling, which is to help women rediscover their voices, gain clarity of purpose, and develop the confidence with which to harness their potential. That is my identity. I have aligned with the people I am called to serve, and I am serving them by being an agent of help to their most pressing problems, which is finding clarity and developing confidence, amongst other things.

So, when I call myself a women capacity builder and a women development strategist, that is who I am. That is my identity, and I tailor my mindset towards uncovering all my ability to become what I have identified for myself. It is the knowledge of myself that guides my journey on becoming phenomenal.

What is your identity? The common interpretation we give to our identity as women is our physical attributes, external validations, recognition, certification, social status, and nationality. Your identity is those intrinsic attributes of your being. They are the unchangeable things about you. If you decide to dump your certificates, change your name from Regina to Chioma, or if something happens and your marital status moves from being married to single or vice versa, does that change who you really are? No. So, your identity is not in the external validations of time, place and people.

Your identity is your core value and belief systems.

What you believe and value is who you are. Do you believe you are a slave? A mediocre? A coward? A queen? That is who you are! Do you value human and animal lives? Do you value excellence, professionalism, or insolence? That is your identity. Your identity is qualified by your value and belief systems and the understanding of your personality.

Your knowledge about yourself, **mindset and identity**, and who you are becoming, **vision and life's purpose**, is the first process to your emergence and becoming phenomenal.

What is your knowledge of your vision?

Vision is a divine, mental preview of coming attraction. It is what you can see today as a potential for your tomorrow. Vision is seeing your tomorrow in the now; bringing tomorrow into the present and living today like you want tomorrow to be. So, journeying the path to becoming phenomenal is to catch a glimpse of your tomorrow, today, and live each day a step towards materializing the picture you have 'envisioned.' Vision is simply a matter of how you see yourself in the future. It is acquiring fresh perspective for your life from God's vantage. To become phenomenal, you must have both seen the journey ahead and knowledgeable about the process of getting there.

Purpose is understanding the essence of your existence; the reason you live, for whom you live, and how you can serve whom you live for. It is a manifestation of what you envision in your journey. Before purpose, there must be vision. You cannot serve who you do not see serving. You cannot become what you can't see. You only become what you see and know and it is in the becoming that purpose is fulfilled.

Purpose is not defined by how people want you to serve them. It is about how you choose to serve. For instance, if I ask about the purpose of a cup I will get numerous responses. Some will say the purpose of a cup is to drink water, others will think it is to drink wine. For some, it is to measure foodstuffs like garri, rice or sugar. You can see that a cup can serve different needs according to the users' objective: whether to drink water, wine or measure stuff. But the activity of the cup is not the sole purpose of a cup. The purpose of a cup is to contain stuff. The user gets to decide what to pour into the cup.

I gave the above illustration to show you that to discover your purpose is not dependent on the crowd. It is not what you should seek from people. Why? People will define who you are and what you are becoming according to their use for you. To leave your journey to becoming phenomenal by external validation or by other people's vision will disengage your process, and becoming it will be you living on their terms – and not on your terms. What this does is that it leaves you at the beck and call of others, doing all things but achieving little or nothing, getting exhausted easily and most likely quit on your journey.

Here are some questions to help you find purpose:

1. What is that problem that drives your passion, triggers a cause to thinking or finding solutions?

2. Who has these problems? The people with those problems are those you are called to serve.

3. Having identified the problem that gives you sleepless nights, the problems that irritate you and spur your interest to correct, or perhaps that experience or challenge you passed through and can successfully help others through

the process, ask yourself, how can you help solve the problem or what can you do to solve the problem?

It could be the problem of rape, divorce, gap in communication, struggle in business, difficult workplace, problem of leadership, a gap in your chosen career path, a gap in ministry, whatever problem irritates you and you know, via experience or advocacy, you can resolve, you know who has this problem and how to solve it, then you've uncovered your knowledge of who you should journey towards becoming.

Again, a major fact worthy of note is that purpose is progressive, as what you think is your journey to becoming phenomenal can take a new turn in a few days, weeks, months or years. It is not static but dynamic and prone to change or adjustments. Your daily experiences and world situations can affect the vision, broaden or narrow it. Whatever the case, it is good you're knowledgeable of the self.

However, it is this first process, self-knowledge, that sets you up on the journey to becoming phenomenal and not normal. Isn't normal boring? Be phenomenal!

THE SYSTEMATIC PROCESS

After arriving at the knowledge of who you are and who you are becoming, the second process or pathway is to be systematic in your daily living. The word here is to become STRATEGIC! How do you achieve the tomorrow you see, solve the problem you have identified, and serve the people you are called to serve if you do not have a well thought out strategy? That is, a sort of daily to-do by which each day gets to become a 'right' step in the direction of realizing and actualizing what and who you envision to become.

Planning: To journey the pathway of becoming phenomenal, you must have plans. One major reason a lot of women find the success of other women challenging and intimidating is that they fail to plan to achieve what they desire out of life. Planning is organized thinking. Brian Tracy once said that most people fail, not because they plan to fail but because they fail to plan. When you discover who you are and whom you are becoming, you realize that organized thinking is key to journeying the path to it. If you want to become the first female president of Nigeria, for instance, but have no plan on how to go about it, it simply becomes a mere wish. Wishes and hopes are not strategies. It is a mere imagination without an organized process to achieving it. Dr. Ngozi Okonjo-Iweala became the first black Director General of the World Trade Organization not by merely wishing but through a systematic process, getting the right education, acquiring the right skills and competencies, serving in various purpose-driven capacities, networking and associating with the right people, gaining the right information, and shooting for the position she envisioned. Today, she has 'become' the first black woman DG of WTO because she planned for it. The world best female tennis player, Serena Williams, keeps bagging awards and jewels and is globally celebrated not because she merely wished to become the world best, but consistent practice and planning led her through what she has become and still becoming.

Dear woman, what vision do you have for yourself? What purpose or assignment are you called into? And what plans are you making to journey through the process to becoming it?

As a women development strategist and clarity coach, I have found out that the reason women are stuck in the ordinary is because we do not know how to plan. When I work with clients on helping them birth purpose, the greatest challenge is how to harness the potential to live purposefully, which is on being systematic and planning out best ways to walk the journey through.

Remember, becoming phenomenal is a journey and requires organized thinking. So let's think together.

Here's a systematic formula to help you plan:
Step One: Decide on who you are becoming

The starting point for planning is an intentional decision. If you have a vision and you are confident in the assignment you are called into, decide exactly what you want to achieve. It may be advocating for rape victim survivors, furthering your career, getting married, etc., whatever it is, just ensure you're not been limited by not planning. Intentionally spell out who you are becoming: an agriculturalist, an author, a marriage counselor, a relationship expert, world best chef, award-winning skater. Be specific, name it, and decide on the goal.

Step Two: Write down your objectives and your compelling why

When the reason for something is unknown, abuse becomes inevitable. Spell out the reasons for which you are journeying the path to becoming phenomenal. Until you can carefully narrate your why, you can plan all there is to achieving your vision and still fall by the wayside. Why? Because there is no compelling force to why you should be extraordinary. You will remain comfortable in your rest zone and won't see reasons to stretch yourself to the limits. One question people often ask me is why I do what I do, why I chose to journey the path of women development strategist. My strong why is something I share on all platforms when I speak or consult: my late mother's philosophy, *"Nwanyi bu uru"* – meaning, a woman is an asset. And that's my compelling why! Growing up in a patriarchal society that confined the lives of women to reproductive and home keeping functions, my late mother's experience, birthing more of girls in such society, made her resolve to rewrite the narrative of women being seen as liabilities, by ensuring she led us along the right path, and having us realize that a woman is first "human" before "woman." Hence, I took the baton from her to finish the race of helping other women rediscover the power in their voices, uncover their abilities, and harness their potentials, as they are more and have more to offer to their world. My compelling force is: An empowered woman, empowers women.

Did you find my WHY compelling? That is the reason I show up every day on my Facebook community, **Capacity Building Network**, inspiring and challenging women and teaching them the right principles by which to improve their minds and skills. It is for this reason I founded the organization, **Dare Women for Change Initiative**, a non-profit and a skill-based platform on a mission to educate and empower the girl-child and young women to dare to be more through mentorship, educational support and advocacy, to evolve and get involved. It is for this same reason that I wrote this book, to cause an awakening in your mind to see yourself as a future forward female and a phenomenal.

What is your why on journeying the path to becoming phenomenal? Until you decide and write it down, you cannot develop the goals you want to achieve. Your why could be to inspire lives, to break the jinx of fewer women in your workplace, to reduce the menace of sexual violence, to stop corruption in Nigeria, to improve the leadership situation of the country, to birth innovative technologies that will enhance human lives, etc. Whatever it is, I need you to know that that is what will sustain the confidence with which you are on the journey.

Step Three: Write down goals

List out all the goals you wish to achieve as a phenomenal. Every week, I write down my goals and the result is visible. Without goals, *becoming* is impossible. Can you imagine if there were no lawn tennis court for Serena Williams, the world best Tennis player, to showcase her skills? There would not have been any phenomenal Serena. It is because there is a tennis court and there are players for her to compete with, that is why she is world best. For instance, my goal is to at least reach out to two women weekly, who will be inspired either through my write ups, my personality or a one-on-one encounter with them, where they get to seeing that there is more to them being women. But how can I achieve this goal if there is no social media or other platforms to leverage?

Matter-of-factly, without goals and definite plans to achieve them, there is no becoming. You will live each day without vision, purpose, why, or goal for your life, and keep complaining about the success of others, especially women. So, what are your financial, personal development, spiritual, career goals? Write them out and make definite plans for achieving them.

Step Four: Develop a detailed plan for achieving your goals

By detailed plan here I mean, leveraging the skills and tools you need to achieve your goals. Produce a detailed plan of the services you want to offer, the problems you want to solve, the career level you want to attain, the income you want to make from that business, etc. This is very important because it helps you check where you have gaps and how to bridge them. Decide what to give to get what you want. And if you do not have the required skills to match who you are becoming, decide to acquire it. Attend that course or become an apprentice, get the certification, plan the conference, attend the seminar, the workshop, the training, get the testimonials, and ensure to steadily hammer yourself into the character of who you are becoming. In developing this detailed plan, give yourself a timeline/deadline. A goal and plan without a deadline can be compared to mere hopes and wishes. Attaching deadlines, which is a confirmed timeframe to achieve a task, makes becoming phenomenal a worthwhile journey and dynamic process.

THE SOCIAL KNOWLEDGE PROCESS

This is the knowledge you have about your personality. The journey of becoming does not end with identifying purpose and serving the people you are called to serve. There is more to it. It equally entails social knowledge, which is knowledge about one's personality, knowledge of people management, how to act, react, and relate with people with a view to collaboration and progress. It is knowledge of your self-esteem and confidence. In simple terms, social knowledge is personality development, which is about the whole makeup of a person. In this pathway, we will start with understanding your temperament, and then learn how to work and live with people without chaos or controversy.

I'll explain this process extensively in the key to aligning and sustaining your phenomenal journey as a woman walking the path of purpose and not an ordinary life.

Having outlined the pathways to becoming phenomenal, there could still be webs and lenses that hinder women from journeying the path of phenomenal and it is pertinent to examine them.

Signposts that limit women on becoming phenomenal

These are lenses through which most women view their lives and those of others, that raise chaos, bickering, unhealthy competition, and fear, amongst others, and frighten the boldness of the few who dare step forward into a phenomenal life.

The past: When we let terrible experiences, poor relationships, betrayal, infidelity, sexual abuse, or hurtful memories get to us, we often conclude that those experiences will influence who we are becoming. You might have been bruised by your experiences. It could be an ugly experience from your relationship, family or friends. Such a situation can rubbish your self-esteem and give you the feeling of worthlessness. A heartbreak, betrayal or backstab can make you feel low and look like a shadow of yourself. This could hugely rob you of confidence, affect your energy level and desire to be more in life.

While working with women, I have had clients who desired to be more but were held back by memories of their past lives. A typical example is a lady who, after an abortion that almost claimed her life, turned to serve God and had wanted to use her social platform as a crusade to reach out to young girls by sharing Christian and religious materials on her page. But on a second thought she felt it is hypocrisy to preach against the flirty lifestyle she was formerly into. Sadly, she was viewing her new life and transformed self through the lens of her past, and was judging the vision and purpose she had based on her former lifestyle. Seeing your journey through the lens of the past will limit your zeal to journey the path to becoming phenomenal, regardless. Let the past live in the past, and should not interrupt your future vision and dreams. To err is human and to forgive is divine. Forgive your past and forge on to glory.

Family upbringing: Family is the foremost determinant of who and what a woman becomes. It is basically what forms our ideology and thought patterns as women. Family informs us about culture, shapes our identity, forms our interpersonal relationships and, to a greater extent, forms our belief system.

Families vary in the sort of training they give to their wards. These pieces of training develop your outcome and potential output. While some people grow up in families where their opinions and suggestions are not sought for during decision-making, some others are given the freedom to make choices as well as express their opinions on decisions made about them.

For instance, child A's parents are learned and always seek her opinion over issues about her welfare. They discipline to correct and not instill fear in the child, hence child A feels comfortable and eloquent enough to communicate her feelings. Child B's parents are also learned but always hush him when he wants to express his feelings. They correct him in a judgmental and condemnable way, "You can never get anything right," "You're dumb," "You are a fool," and such hurting words. This kind of discipline registers in child B's subconscious and makes him develop the fear of expressing himself in words and action. This will eventually plunge child B into the abyss of low self-confidence.

Child B never experienced the freedom to share his fears or discuss his needs, as everything was parent-imposed. This indirectly reduces the level of expression of the child, as he'd most naturally find it difficult to share his thoughts amongst his peers. So, when a family shows little or no care and gives no attention to the growing child, it often inhibits the child's self-confidence, leads to low self-esteem and inhibits the desire to grow above family expectations.

Environment: The nature-nurture debate is an age-long one. Psychologists have remained at loggerheads as to what exactly informs human behaviour, nature or nurture. That notwithstanding, the environment is known to play a great role in the outcome of one's becoming desires. By environment, I mean the neighbourhood and group of friends one associates with. If you live or lived in neighbourhoods that are cynical to your growth, you either were chastised for your physical features (looks, height or weight) or were taken for granted and seen as one who won't amount to anything, then you can attest to how much damage that is capable of. Such name calling, in most cases, takes a huge toll on your subconscious, such that you start to live according to other people's narratives about you. This is the reality and the major reason women battle with lack of vision and low self-confidence. I recall the story of a young woman who was chastised for her height. She was called short and all sorts of names to rubbish her self-esteem. She then grew up thinking everything was about her height until she had a mental surgery, one that allowed her to see her good sides. She was an excellent communicator, with people always asking her to represent them in group presentations, not minding her height. She only feels adequate when she is functioning in the speaking space and has capitalized on her strength, which is speaking, to train over a hundred individuals on how to become effective communicators in her speaking academy. You see, the environment almost messed her up.

Fear: Fear is a major factor that hinders people from living their best lives and confidently so. It is a mental construct that instigates a feeling of powerlessness. Truth is, the things the mind imagine when it fears are largely untrue. Most people have a fear of not speaking correct grammar, fear of how people will perceive them —people syndrome, fear of failure, fear of not making a good impression after carrying out a task or responsibility, the I-can't-do-it mindset.

And this brings me to ask, why be afraid of what you don't know? The outcome of whatever you're afraid of can only be ascertained when you give it a try. Moreover, failure is only what you get when you fail and refuse to get back on your feet. But when you see failure as merely a feedback with which to get right the things you did wrong, you will always triumph.

Comparison: Comparison is insecurity, and insecurity is a self-battle. You're constantly battling with yourself over what and how you should feel. To kill insecurity, you must understand that perfection is an illusion. Imperfection is part of life. So, stop comparing yourself and wishing to be like others. Appreciate your imperfections and function in them.

Self-Labels: I have heard women label themselves all sorts of things just to keep to normal, including: "I am a private person," "I am introverted," "I am shy." I can't help but laugh at these labels. When you affirm such to yourself, what you actually do is align yourself to your limiting beliefs, thus excusing yourself to remain normal. Conditioning your mind to see only the negatives and impossibilities, these self-labels get to hinder your growth process.

Dear woman, trash the self-imposed labels and assume an epic life for yourself, one of becoming more.

Consequently, the same signposts or lenses, depending on the turn-out of events, can also impact one's level of confidence. A good family background can raise an individual's level of confidence. If your parents are such that allow you to freely express your opinions and make choices, you unconsciously grow up exhibiting a high desire to dare to become more. Likewise, your environment, if enabled with trust, guidance, positivity, acceptance, freedom of expression, appreciation of your abilities, love and care, will tend to polish your confidence. Again, your experiences can help you muster confidence in yourself. Your life experiences, if filled with sweet memories, can help you channel your inner strength to achieve more than your weakness would ever deprive you of.

So, you see how the same factors that make a thing can also mar its effectiveness. All the determinants we've seen above are parallels and, depending on the context and perspective of usage, have the power to inhibit your desire to become phenomenal.

There are tons of limiting lenses we wear which clog our reasoning and thinking, and if I am to list all in details, trust me, I'll have to write an entirely new book. However, I know for sure that the lenses identified above will give you a guide to call your limitations by name. So, look at the ones mentioned above and add yours.

What are they?

CHAPTER FOUR

UNBUNDLING CONFIDENCE

"The quality of your life cannot be better than the quality of information available to you."

~Sam Adeyemi

* * *

SCREW ENVY. EMBRACE CONFIDENCE.

If there's anything I know from my years of existence as a woman, it is that women prefer keeping males as best friends. And to be fair, this is not without a good reason. When you see a human being preferring another race, gender or tribe over theirs, then you should know that they must have a good reason for it, especially when it is common amongst all the people in that class.

From both my findings and experience, one reason many women prefer male friends to female friends is because of the stories of betrayal, rivalry, and mistrust they have heard – or experienced. I use the word "heard" because most times, the women with more male friends haven't really had sour experiences with females. They just take their time to observe the relationship women have with other women, and then decide it's not for them. Some heard these stories as kids, and from that stage already look forward to the evil in fellow women. The truth is that, if you walk around with a hammer you would most likely see nails where there aren't any. By holding on to the wrong perception that women are their own enemies, women tend to walk around seeing the wrongs in other women, even when there isn't necessarily anything to be wary of. It's simply a problem of mindset. Looking at it carefully, it is not unconnected with lack of personal trust and self-confidence.

Realistically, lack of confidence is the reason many women are quick to dish out judgments and condemnations against one another. You might be tempted to think that it is because the other person is actually wrong or bad, but if you take time to consider the root of the person's bitterness or anger, you would see that it stems from a lack of confidence.

This topic of confidence is one many shy away from. And the failure to engage in discussions about this serves to perpetuate the rancour amongst women. How did I know this? Through the course of my work with women as a women development strategist, I understand how essential it is for the subject on confidence to be explored, as it is a major root of the chaotic nature of womanhood, amongst other things. Most women lack the sincerity to look beyond their weaknesses to see the profound strengths domiciled in them. They doubt their abilities and are held in fear of living below the highlights of the other women, and below the standard set for her by society.

Working with women has given me ample opportunity to interact with and listen to women from different walks of life. As a development coach, I help women gain clarity of life's purpose and develop the confidence to harness potentials for personal growth and societal relevance. My experiences with these women are something I hold so dear. It continues to inspire and challenge me to do and be more. Also, as the lead volunteer in my non-profit (Dare Women for Change Initiative), I have continued to observe that the major challenge of most women is lack of confidence. They lack personal confidence in themselves and in the possibility of their becoming. When assignments that require public exposure or in-house presentation are given, volunteers shy away with the excuse of lack of confidence to face the crowd or speak in public. By the way, our mission as an organization is to empower, educate, and equip women with the necessary skillset to evolve and get involved in nation-building through the provision of literacy tools, mentorship, coaching, and empowerment programmes. The question of confidence is so vital for the phenomenal woman that it is irreplaceable.

Confidence is the basis for revamping and reorienting the mentality of women to understand the power in supporting one another. And it is essential that the awakening or orientation starts with women learning to develop unmatched confidence. One brilliant strategy to the part of becoming phenomenal sustainably is in mastering CONFIDENCE. It is the key to unlocking the greatest potential, uncovering your strength, ending intra-gender war, and outshining one's old self.

This book's purpose is to establish confidence as the key to becoming phenomenal, address the issues surrounding lack of confidence, and show how women can develop high self-confidence, which will help curb the unhealthy rivalry and bane of womanhood presented in chapter one, while living a phenomenal life.

The point is, no matter how much of a life of purpose and influence you desire to live, you cannot thrive without a good dose of confidence. It is confidence that helps you kickstart and sustain the journey of becoming phenomenal.

CONFIDENCE MYTHS

These myths were introduced by people, propagated by people, and ultimately promoted by people – and have become even more popular and widely accepted than the real deal. Before we dive into what confidence truly is, and how to build up one's confidence as a phenomenal woman, it would make sense to identify the confidence myths.

Confidence is hereditary

This is one of the biggest and most controversial myths of confidence. We have been taught to see confidence as a genetic material passed down from parents to offspring. This myth suggests that confidence cannot be built or developed; it can only be inherited. Which implies that if you're not fortunate enough to have parents who are confident, then you can kiss confidence goodbye in yourself. This further implies that confident people have always had confidence running in their lineage – and the same for those who lack confidence. Thankfully, this is never the case. Science has not classified or proven confidence as a hereditary material— at least, as at the time of this publication. So, one does not become confident, act confident, or believe in his abilities because they inherited the genes of confidence from a parent or grandparent. Confidence is, strictly speaking, an acquired trait. It does not come by inheritance but by careful insistence. The wise man, Alexander Graham Bell, once said, "A man, as a general rule, owes very little to what he is born with—a man is what he makes of himself." This quote from Alexander clearly dissolves the myth that confidence is hereditary. Confidence is not in the genes. You are ultimately responsible for what you become irrespective of how and where you were born. A man is what he makes of himself, and not necessarily what his parents or dominant and recessive genes make of him. As women, we don't develop confidence automatically. There are factors which come into play to manifest these things.

Confidence is natural

This is one misconception that has chained many women for decades. Some think that it is not in their nature to be confident, that they are not born with that feature. But I've got news for you. In the theory of knowledge, the empiricist philosopher John Locke maintains that the mind is a "tabula rasa" at birth. This means that, the human mind is a blank slate at birth and only receives and understands data or information as a result of its experience and exposure to its environment and other determining factors of life. So, everyone is born as a blank slate. This goes to suggest that no human is born with confidence or without it. It is simply a feature in us that we can choose to activate or allow to lie dormant. Confidence is not a natural gift. Human beings grow through the phases of life and experiences into becoming confident by conscious and unconscious effort. For instance, when a child is born, it is natural that he goes through the developmental stages. She learns to sit, crawl, stand, and before long she can walk and even run. This explains different stages of her growth process. In the same vein, one has to "grow" confidence over time.

Confidence is being loud

Being loud doesn't translate to confidence. That you try to manipulate situations using your voice at its loudest pitch does not mean you are confident. There's a thick line between exuding high confidence and being an empty barrel. Loudness is mostly associated with uncouth, nasty, uncivil, and often unruly behaviour. Confidence speaks value, purpose, civility and impact. However, the line between loudness and confidence can be found in the content, information, value and composure displayed in verbal or non-verbal communication. Most people fear silence because it leaves them vulnerable. Confidence is you speaking when necessary and communicating your point in a manner your audience can clearly understand.

Confidence is eloquence

Part of the lies we have believed, part of the deceit that's burdened many of us and even buried some of us is the idea that confidence is equal to eloquence or fluency in speech. Let me say here that one does not necessarily need to know all the big words in the dictionary to become confident. That you are an expert doesn't translate to being confident. For instance, a chartered accountant might get nervous when called upon to make a financial statement presentation, even with all his knowledge of financial jargons. Likewise, a religious leader might get nervous before mounting the pulpit to minister to his congregation. A teacher could sometimes develop chills when she's about to teach. So, being an expert does not translate to confidence. Again, being a fast talker does not equate with confidence. That you can speak a thousand words in one minute does not make you confident. What is the need of rushing your words and not communicating? There is more to confidence than meets the eye. You'll find out real soon.

Confidence is arrogance

There's confidence, and then there's arrogance. Confidence is not arrogance! Being arrogant means showcasing an exaggerated sense of one's importance or abilities. Arrogance is the feeling of superiority above others. For instance, a student who is best in class may belittle her fellow students' abilities because of her academic prowess. Her conversations about being the best in class are often done to spite or send wrong signals. She uses curse words to describe others, making them feel less of themselves. That is arrogance. And arrogance is not confidence. Confidence does not elevate a person's image at the expense of another. Confidence protects itself and others; it does not harm or damage another's self-esteem, but elevates it. Confidence inspires confidence in others. It does not provoke timidity or a feeling of worthlessness in another. Confidence will always empower and enliven every spirit it comes in contact with. Often, we address ambitious, woke, and informed people who are making genuine progress in their fields as confident people, even when they are insolent and rude in relating or managing relationships. Confidence is not being disrespectful or boastful and should not be likened to such. Confidence is not pride. It shows respect and honor for the other and not self-seeking.

Those are some of the myths we have long harboured in our minds about confidence. And they have hindered and resisted our rising as phenomenal women of influence. We must intentionally discard them and imbibe true confidence. The phenomenal lady must grow beyond these myths and realize that confidence is positive, desirable and beneficial to everyone. It is a fragrance that she can wear without suffocating other women around her.

Having walked the path of a shy and nervous lady in the past and improved on my search for and level of confidence, I can categorically say that lack of confidence persists because women lack the right information as to what it truly means to be confident. The misconceptions that confidence is hereditary, natural, divinely orchestrated, etc., is the reason most ladies attribute their fears and inability to face life challenges to lack of confidence.

One thing to note is that the concept of confidence is an encompassing subject. By definition, it has a large range of meaning, as it is used in different contexts to connote different things. In a personality context, confidence is defined as the composure and reflection of one's behaviour, attitude and reactions to things. It reflects how one walks, talks, sits, and relates with people.

Confidence is commonly attributed to being fearless, bold, and possessing the ability to easily and freely express one's self. I carried out a poll some time ago in my Facebook community, **Capacity Building Network**, asking to know the opinion of women on what confidence means, and the majority concluded that confidence means boldness in one's ability, self-love, and positive-mindedness.

I like to define confidence as the ability to understand one's weaknesses, limitations and shortcomings, and yet know how to make it up using one's strength. In any context of description, the two underlying basis for confidence is knowing your "weakness" and using your "strength" against the weakness. For instance, a lady who is introverted might make the excuse that she does not need jobs that would project her on spotlight. But this same lady has such excellent communication skills. Hence, with a job in a financial institution, where she would meet most of her prospects one-on-one, this lady can allow her conversational self—the part of her that loves to engage in conversations with people—to have a greater part of her job than her introverted self.

CONFIDENCE FOR A PHENOMENAL WOMAN

A phenomenal understands confidence as the ability to stop trying to do things one doesn't have the capacity for. She understands confidence as finding her place of strength and engaging life from there.

Confidence is a skill

From the above definition, one can say that **Confidence is a skill** that needs to be mastered. It is a skill because it can be learned. Anything that is not natural is learned, and anything learned is a capability or a skill. Confidence, as a skill, entails the mastery of one's strength and knowing when to deploy it against one's weakness. And the beauty of this is that skill can be mastered with experience and deliberate practice. So, we all grow up learning to become confident, for nobody is born confident.

Ask yourself this question: what are my shortcomings, weaknesses, or limitations? And what are my strengths? Take some time and think this through. Then get a notebook and write down your answers. If you can really identify these things, boom! Your journey to developing unmatched confidence becomes easier and more interesting.

For instance, if you stammer while speaking, you can learn breath control and the use of pauses in speech to overcome the stammering limitation and speak more confidently. That is confidence, learning to upturn your weakness, using your strength. If this can be learned, then confidence is a skill.

Confidence is a mindset

You must dig deep into yourself to draw confidence. Confidence is your ability to have an open mind, to handle anything, such as work, family, social events or relationships, without a fear of uncertainty. As ladies, we exist more in a physical world and are prone to spending a lot of our time looking on the outside to find confidence. We look to derive confidence in the clothes we wear, the number of accessories we put on, and the number of compliments we receive from friends and strangers. And when our expectations aren't met, we slip into a shadow of ourselves. We think ourselves worthless and feel defeated even in our strengths. Always remember, "As a woman thinks in her heart, so is she." Your current level is a manifestation of all thoughts in your mind.

Confidence is commitment

When you don't define confidence as a step to success, it cripples you from having your visions and goals met. The problem is not that you lack confidence to dare your goals. The first thing to launch is not confidence but commitment. Until you are committed to achieving your goals, until your mind is made up on getting something done, confidence will be far from your dwelling. It is the commitment you have to do a thing that drives your confidence out on the scene. With commitment, your strength rises over your weakness and overshadows it. Until you are intentional about a responsibility or task, until you dare your guts to make it happen by engaging focus and exercising control over your body, you are never confident.

So, you see that confidence is often overrated. It is not the first thing you see when you are about to take action, but commitment. It is commitment that interprets intentionality and fuels your ability to use your strength over your weakness. Thus, when you sit around and only decide to apply all the tips shared on how to develop confidence or wish you can take up responsibilities as others do, and yet not commit to taking action, you miss the whole point. I'm sorry to disappoint you, confidence will be far from your dwelling if you don't decide to apply the tips we've shared here, beyond just reading and nodding in affirmation to the truth they embody. As much as you decide to develop confidence, you must be committed and disciplined to put into practice every additional information you gather. Your next phase is dependent of your new level of information.

From the examined definitions of confidence above, you can clearly see that no one is born confident. Same way every baby cries at birth, everyone once had confidence in short supply. The cry of the baby implied a call for help and assistance, and then he/she grows through life stages, able to manage things for him/herself – and the crying becomes less and less. Same applies to confidence. Nobody is born confident, but our experience, decisions and commitment grow our ability to handle things on our own without needing a third party push or external motivation. That is Confidence!

Simply put, confidence is not an end, it is a process and a means to an expected end.

A phenomenal lady who understands confidence will thrive when others are struggling. She clearly sees that confidence is a mindset, a skill, and a process that can be learned through determination and focus. It is this knowledge of confidence that opens your learning spirit and helps you cope with mistakes when you fail and need to try again. Confidence changes the way you view things and interpret life's situations. You see possibility regardless of the situation you are facing because you know you are learning a skill. To have unmatched confidence is to understand that human beings are fallible; anyone can make a mistake. So, you take responsibility for your mistakes and strive to grow and get better. Confidence makes you not to give up on yourself or feel embarrassed when you make mistakes or commit a blunder. You don't drown yourself in self-pity and regrets. You simply adjust your poise, pick up the lessons, and take another step with boldness.

I shall painstakingly expose the qualities you need to imbibe in order to develop unmatched confidence. Let's see some of the features and traits of unmatched confidence, the kind you need to possess as a phenomenal lady.

CHAPTER FIVE

FEATURES OF AN UNMATCHED CONFIDENCE

*"It is confidence in our bodies, minds, and spirits that allows
us to keep looking for new adventures."*
~ Oprah Winfrey

* * *

Confidence is a major requirement to becoming, but developing unmatched confidence will lead you through the epic process of becoming phenomenal. Women who are able to build unmatched confidence end up having an irresistible personality, one that marks them out as legends. I will take a cue from the life of legendary and outstanding, world-celebrated women to describe the characteristics of a woman with unmatched confidence. You should personalize these processes and channel them towards your life. Dr. Ngozi Okonjo Iweala, Serena Williams, Maya Angelou, Michelle Obama, Amina of Zaria, etc., all pursued different fields and career paths but had the following features in common:

Intentionality

A woman with unmatched confidence is intentional about her daily living. She lives to bring good and not evil to herself and her household. Intentionality in choices, associations, and information. (Proverbs 31:12 says, "she will do him good and not evil all the days of her life.")

Resourcefulness

A woman with unmatched confidence is resourceful and hardworking. She works to make a living and a name for herself as a brand or an entrepreneur. (Proverbs 31:13 tells us that "She seeks wool and flax and works willingly with her hands." Verse 16 continues, "She considers a field, and buys it: with the fruits of her hands she plants a vineyard." And in verse 24, "She makes fine clothes and sells it; and delivers girdles unto the merchant." Verse 27b gives a graphic description of her resourcefulness: "She does not eat the bread of idleness.")

Standards

A woman with unmatched confidence has core values and is principled. She is one with defined standards and not the anything-goes kind of person. She believes in something and promotes it. It could be excellence, integrity, good leadership, etc. Her standards are values that make her exceptional. At the mention of the thing, they are outlined to fill in the gap. (Proverbs 25 says, "Strength and honor are her clothing and she shall rejoice in time to come.")

Family-inclined

A woman of unmatched confidence knows how to balance family with business or career. She loves herself, her family and her God, and does not prioritize one over the other. She pays attention and takes care of her family, regardless of her career or business advancement. She does not pursue one to the peril of the other.

There's a balance and that you must learn. (Proverbs 31:15, "She rises also while it is yet night, and gives meat to her household, and a portion to her maidens." Verse 22 says, "She is not afraid of the snow for her household: for all her household are clothed with scarlet." And verse 27a tells us that "She looks well to the ways of her household.")

Good dress sense

A lady with unmatched confidence understands, as a rule of thumb, how not to dress like her mates. Instead, she dresses like where she is going to and how she wants to be addressed. She does not dress shabbily or casually. She dresses and adorns herself with fine clothing, laced with great poise and character. (Proverbs 31:22 says, "She makes herself coverings of tapestry; her clothing is silk and purple.")

Full of wit

Such a woman with unmatched confidence is very brilliant. She is an avid and voracious reader and speaks with so much wisdom and information. She knows a thing about everything and is acquainted with the happenings in her environment and abroad. (Proverbs 26, "She opens her mouth with wisdom.")

Fearless/daring

She is fearless and dares her guts, facing situations as they present themselves. She is committed to standing up for whatever she believes is right. She is bold and courageous. (Verse 14 confirms that "She is like the merchant ships; she brings food from afar." And in verse 17, "She girded her loins with strength and strengthened her arms.")

Empathic

A woman of unmatched confidence is not arrogant. Rather, she is filled with compassion and empathy. She feels the grief or happiness of another and shares in it. Her heart is saturated with kindness and she reaches out to everyone who comes into her circle. (Verse 20 says, "She stretches out her hand to the poor; yea, she reaches forth her hands to the needy." And verse 26 adds that, "She opens her mouth with wisdom, and in her tongue is the law of kindness.")

Innovative and Creative

This woman is innovative and creative. She has the ability to turn new and imaginative ideas into reality. She's always excited in exploring and trying out new things that elevate her growth. (Verses 18 and 19 says, "She elevates her growth." Verses 18 and 19 says, "She perceives that her merchandise is good: her candle goes not out by night; she lays her hands to the spindle, and her hands hold the distaff.")

Self-control

The woman with unmatched confidence has control over her emotions and knows how to relate and live with people. She is not dependent or over expectant of other people.

Interest

A phenomenal woman has an exceptional interest in a particular area. She understands she's been called to shine her light to the world, and therefore uses her gifts, experience, talents or skills to serve her world. She is knowledgeable of what her calling is, and she graceful responds to her call to serve.

Planning

A phenomenal woman has her life figured out to an extent. She knows her journey and process to becoming and plans her life, living each day a step closer to her aspirations.

Mentors

While reading the biography of most of the outstanding, phenomenal women, one thing is certain: they all strived to learn and persist in learning. Mentors make the journey faster. They are the shoulders you could gladly lean on to foresee your journey of becoming and take the right direction in the process. There is something I call the cheat code of mentorship. Study them, read their biographies, buy their resources, research their interests, their likes, their dislikes, understand what they value and believe in. It will guide you through your process and journey of becoming.

Above all, a woman who possesses unmatched confidence is conscious of what I call the 4Bs of womanhood: **Beauty, Boldness, Brilliance and Background.** Let's look at each of these 4Bs closely:

Beauty

This is an emphasis on her awareness that she's truly beautiful in her form, regardless of societal definition of beauty. This implies that whether you are tall, short, average, fair, dark, slim or fat, you are beautiful in your own right. You are not defined by the conventional beauty of the media because "beauty is in the beholder's eye" – and what you behold about yourself is who you are and what truly matters. This positive mentality about your looks boosts your confidence.

Boldness

This emphasizes your ability to trust yourself to rise up to the occasion with positivity. You are not afraid of whatever comes your way, but you make headway with your guts. This is understanding that whatever challenge that faces you will require your effort alone to surmount. Nobody is coming to save or help you. It's up to you, and your mindset is key to standing up or speaking up for yourself.

Brilliance

A confident woman is versatile in knowledge. She is never caught unawares. She's a good reader and a good speaker. Her words and ideas flow easily when she speaks because her mind is conditioned to interpret what has been stored up in her subconscious. Brilliance will always separate you from the rest of the pack. Because you know more, your perspective is always different. And this results from your constant upgrade with information. In brilliance, you see problems as opportunities and only envisage solutions.

Background

This emphasis on your awareness that a human being is not defined by where he is coming from. You are not defined by the wealth or wretchedness of your family. Your reality should not be a function of your family circumstance. You don't allow thoughts about your background to limit you or stop you from dreaming big.

A woman's awareness of these 4Bs of womanhood removes the spike of ignorance for confidence to reign.

CHAPTER SIX

STEPS TO DEVELOP UNMATCHED CONFIDENCE

"When you have a lot of confidence and you feel like nobody can beat you, it's game over for everyone else."

~ Jason Day

* * *

Confidence is beautiful to wear. It is one thing that can make you stand out from your peers and colleagues if you know how to wear it correctly. Like Marcus Garvey rightly pointed out, "With confidence, you have won before you have started." Indeed, everyone must desire to build unmatched confidence, one that can open people's hearts even when their doors have been shot.

Confidence is as important to becoming phenomenal as oxygen is to breathing. The good news is that women who are outstanding are not born with confidence. It is not a matter of genetics. We can improve and build on it.

I like to state that the tips shared herein on how to develop unmatched confidence is not a Ponzi scheme or a get-confident-quick formula. Remember, confidence is a skill acquired with the right mindset through practice and commitment. It was Barrie Davenport who said, "Low-self-confidence is not a life sentence. Self-confidence can be learned, practiced and mastered, just like any other skill. Once you master it, everything in your life will change for the better."

Here are tips to guide you through developing unmatched confidence:

Eliminate triggers: Avoid negative thinking or spending time around things that make you feel bad about yourself. These triggers may be people, places, or situations. As best as you can, eliminate them around you. If they are friends, cut them off. Evaluate your circle and surround yourself with people who believe in you, inspire you to be bold and adventurous.

Embrace your flaws: Your limitations and weaknesses are part of who you are. You need to understand this to grow from a place of fear to faith, and fully trust your abilities. Understand that no human is perfect. It is foolishness to think someone out there has got his or her shit all figured out. To develop confidence, you must stop striving for perfection. It is delusional. Embrace and acknowledge your weakness, as that's the only way to work on it using your strength. I doubt if this could have been better said: "Confidence comes not from always being right but from not fearing to be wrong," Peter T. McIntyre.

Live in gratitude: Gratitude multiplies, ingratitude diminishes. You must learn to live daily in gratitude. Learn to say thank you, smile often, and stay cheerful. It exudes positive energy that attracts people to you and boosts your trust in your ability. This effortlessly allows you to take up responsibility with an open mind.

Celebrate your big and small wins: Always give yourself credit for the work you do. The best applause and validation is the one you give yourself. Cheer yourself in your small or big wins and pat yourself at the back for taking up courage to finish a task or conclude a responsibility. What it does is that it boosts your confidence to do more and be more.

Learn from confident people: Look at the people you respect and admire who are doing outstanding things in their different fields, identify what it is they do differently that conveys confidence and check to see what you can learn from them. Don't copy them, but remodel their activities to suit your journey.

Give yourself to service: To develop unmatched confidence, start by availing yourself of possible and practical platforms that can boost your ability to manage your strengths over your weaknesses. Join social clubs or organizations like Rotary International and Toastmasters International. They are speaking and leadership clubs that help you boost your confidence. Or you can join departments in your church or at your workplace. You can volunteer to humanitarian organizations or NGOs. And when you do, take up responsibilities; do not shy away from duty or delegation. It is in doing so that you groom yourself. Confidence comes from discipline and training.

Practice breathing control: When there's a need to show your ability and you're scared, practice breathe control. Put your hands directly under your breast region, keep your eyes closed, and take a deep breath in, and then breathe out. (You can try it now and see how it feels. Try it, did you feel anything? Good.)

The same manner in which you tuck in your belly when walking on the road or about to snap pictures, you can practice breath control to develop confidence.

Breathing is magical. We breathe our thoughts. So, whenever you find yourself nervous about expressing yourself, take a deep breath while your hands are on your stomach, and then breathe out.

Let me share a quick trick with you. When you get into a room and you want to know the confident ones, just check their breathing patterns. The low-confident women breathe fast, feel and look unsettled. And because human beings are emotional and instinctive beings, in a pack of many, the ones who exhibit calm breathing pattern are seen as confident and are the ones who are usually put in charge of situations. So, you see why you should master this act?

Master your underdog tactics: Underdog tactics is simply the ability to know your weaknesses and how to find a way around it using your competence and strengths. It is about what makes you unique from every other person. The underdog tactics in simple terms suggest, "Do what works for you." For instance, if you're not used to waking up by five in the morning to start your day, don't do it because others are doing it. If your wake up time 6am, or even 7, wake up, but make sure you utilize your time very well during the day. It's just like saying, if you are the type that can't read all night but have found out you are more productive during the day, utilize the day well; read, carry out necessary tasks and assignments, and then sleep at night. Mastering what works for you and using it against what might be conventional helps you develop self-confidence.

On doing what works for you, let's take a cue from the story of David and Goliath. From the war front episode, we see that David understood his underdog tactics. He could not fight Goliath with a sword and armor, so he channeled his strength to the use of his sling, the catapult. In history, we read that flying slings or catapult was a skill that the strongest men possessed. David had the job of tending his father's sheep, and when danger struck, he rescued the sheep from its prey with the use of his catapult. Not swords or armors. David understood his strength. And in the face of a similar challenge, a battle against the Philistine, Goliath, he undressed his armor and sword, to fight Goliath and opted instead for his sling. That was a most ridiculous move for the onlookers. But for David, it was the greatest strategy! Even Goliath taunted him, "Am I a dog that you come to me with sticks?" (1 Samuel 17:43). David clearly understood what worked for him and used it. That is what I call mastery of underdog tactics. And so, to become a woman with unmatched confidence, you must identify your underdog tactics and master them! Know what works for you. It could be speaking with highlights written on paper, speaking by heart, reading out an entire speech, whatever works for you, master it and utilize it.

Understand your personality type: To develop unmatched confidence is to understand your personality type. Personality types are the various categories in which psychologists have grouped human behaviour and character. Although there are many personality traits, we shall focus on the most commonly discussed four traits: Sanguine, Melancholy, Choleric and Phlegmatic. These different types are easily described as the playful Sanguine, the perfect Melancholy, the powerful Choleric and peaceful Phlegmatic.

Understanding your personality type and knowing other types helps you to live and work with people in a more comfortable manner, even without prior encounters. It helps you learn to relate with people in a more informed and polished manner.

Let's examine these traits:

*The **playful sanguine**, just as it is called, is the expressive, lively, all time cheerful, adventurous trait. They are creative and fantastic entertainers. However, in their most cheerful state, they are very emotional beings who usually take offense over the simplest of things. They are not good with details because of their playful nature and go throughout the day sharing jabs. They are enthusiastic, love challenges, and are collaborative.

*The **perfect Melancholy** are not the best fun lovers or social beings. This trait can be categorized as the reserved one who loves the company of family and friends and do not necessarily look for adventure outside these. They are orderly and very good with details and are better at administrative and managerial positions. They dislike competitions and are not collaborative.

*The **powerful Choleric** is as powerful as the word attached to it. They are analytical, logical, result-oriented, challenging and dominating. They do enjoy deep and meaningful conversations and love to keep friends with people who are deep in thinking. They get bored with shallow minds easily. Have a mind of their own and not easily discouraged. Because they are firm in their approach, they are usually approached to lead in a pack.

*The **peaceful Phlegmatic** is peaceful, reserved, calm and easygoing. They are good loyalists and would give up anything to avoid chaos or controversy. They look for ways to act as mediators and are comfortable living in their own skin.

People can have more than one personality type. One must be primary and the other secondary. So, it is better you understand your personality type and those of others, as it helps you understand how people think and act, and saves you the stress of always forcing yourself or kind on people. To develop unmatched confidence as a phenomenal, you must operate on this knowledge.

Understand simple social etiquettes: Social etiquettes are polite behavioral patterns that are civil and do not in any form hurt or dehumanize the other. It uplifts the other, and they get to feel important and valuable. When you practice simple etiquettes, it boosts your confidence level; the feeling you get makes you feel pleasant about yourself.

What are these simple etiquettes? Smile often. Greet people aloud with a wide grin. Pass kind remarks and compliments to people. Show gratitude. Use the power words often: "I am sorry, please, excuse me, thank you." Be courteous. Respect people's boundaries and privacy. Treat others as you would like to be treated. These simple acts will greatly boost your confidence and the way you feel about yourself.

Master your genius domain: When people request something of you, they have an assurance and belief that you can do it. One way to quit humiliating yourself unnecessarily is to master your genius domain. Your genius domain is your place of competence. "Believe in yourself! Have faith in your abilities! Without a humble but reasonable confidence in your own powers you cannot be successful or happy"— Norman Vincent Peale.

What is that thing you like to do often? What is your interest, passion or skill? Find it, focus on it, and develop it..Focus is blindness in mastery.

Frankly, "When you have confidence, you can do anything"—Sloane Stevens. Genius domain is not only what you are good at but also what brings out the best in you. Find out what it is and master it. Is it public speaking? Writing? Critical thinking? Analysis? Administration? Whatever it may be, master it. To master your genius domain is to prepare ahead of time so that when opportunity comes you are prepared to deliver.

Be you: Be you and do you. Everyone else is taken. The problem with most women is that we are copycats. We like to copy. Emulation is the best form of flattery, yes. But not when you lose yourself in the process. What you fail to ask yourself is whether you have the same competence as the person you're copying. To develop unmatched confidence, you have to be yourself, be original and maintain your uniqueness. Leverage your competence, as replicas don't sell as high as the original.

Drop the perfectionist mentality: Can you cast your mind back to the analysis of the myth that confidence is hereditary? We established that nobody is born confident; we all grow to learn to be confident. Hence, to develop an unmatched confidence is to understand that nobody is perfect.

And you can't be perfect either, but can strive to become better than you were before. Delete perfection from your dictionary if it has been causing you to take less action. Humans strive to become perfect but cannot attain perfection. When you try new things and fail, see the failure as feedback to right your wrongs. You have got new experience. So, past mistakes become building blocks in recreating another.

For instance, publishers rejected J. K. Rowling, the writer of Harry Potter, 12 times before one publisher finally picked up her script. Today, the movie series has bagged lots of awards and recognition, and is one of the most iconic franchises ever made. Also, the Wright Brothers failed with many models of their aircraft before they succeeded in creating the right aircraft. Studies show that those who fail regularly and keep trying anyway are better equipped to respond to setbacks and challenges constructively. They learn how to ask for strategies, ask others for advice, and persevere in the process. To develop unmatched confidence, you must believe in your ability to improve. Drop the perfectionist mentality, quit overthinking and over planning and start doing. Take massive action. After all, taking action makes the difference between dreamers and inventors.

Hang around people that exude confidence: There is this saying that an expression of someone's feeling and nature triggers the expression of another. Intentionally associate with confident people because such associations are powerful. Vince Lombardi simply had this in mind when he remarked, "Confidence is contagious. So is the lack of it."

Master your C's—Charisma and Control: To develop unmatched confidence, you also need to practice bodily control and poise. This is more about the non-verbal communication discussed in the next point. Your composure is an integral part of your confidence.

Master the use of non-verbal communication: Master the use of non-verbal communication. Nonverbal communication are the unspoken words communicated through body language. This has to do with your sitting, standing and walking positions, how you roll your eyes, how you move your body generally without uttering words. There are high walking, standing and sitting poses, and there are low poses too. The high poses make you appear more confident. For instance, when you walk with your shoulders high and chest out, you are termed confident. This is much unlike a person who walks with shrugged shoulders with face to the ground.

See below some sitting and standing poses:

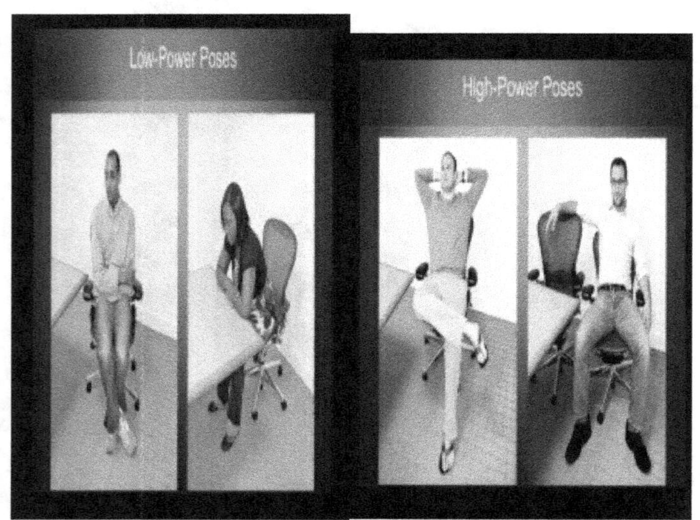
Low-Power Poses
High-Power Poses

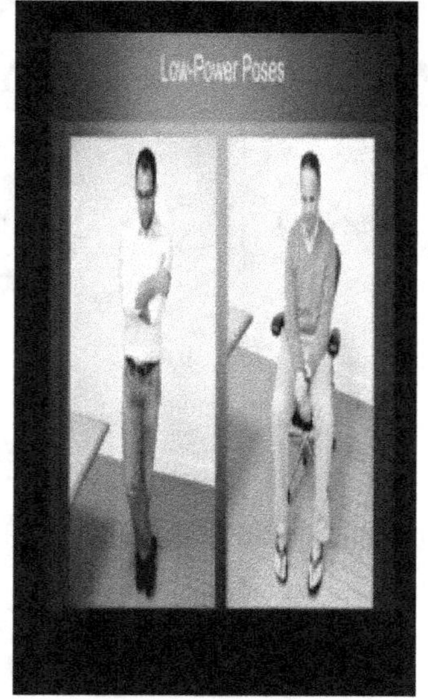
Low-Power Poses

From these images, I guess you can tell the individuals whose body language speaks confidence and boldness, right? You have to always ensure that your body language indicates high power poses; that is, stand heads up, shoulders high, sit upright, legs uptight, facing your conversation partner, maintaining eye contact with an interesting/ cheerful face and not sludging your neck or shoulder when walking, sitting or standing.

Be an avid reader: A woman with unmatchable confidence is value-packed. When you have value to give, expression seems to naturally flow, unlike when you lack content. Being an avid reader will improve your speech mastery. Thus, to develop unmatched confidence is to become a reading disciple. A wise man once said, "The greatest leaders have the best libraries." What are you currently reading? What have you read?

Be a good listener: The ability to listen is one lagging virtue amongst women. To cultivate that unmatched confidence of a phenomenal woman, you must learn to listen and avoid bringing up personal issues when someone is relating their worries. Listening is key to having people trust you and your opinion when it is shared. What being a good listener implies is that you heard and assimilated all that is being said and ordinarily must process the right response. Do not listen to respond, but listen to understand. That sets you apart and endears you to people.

Use positive affirmations: The universe connives with what you affirm and put efforts on. You need to learn the use of positive affirmations. In the place of "cannot," use words like "will" and "shall" to make your affirmations. On a daily, have an affirmation list of positive words that you consciously profess to yourself before setting out for the day. These words will fuel your desire to do more and be more. An instance of positive affirmations is: "I am enough! When my paths cross with people, I speak clarity, I speak solutions. I heal, restore and mend broken hearts with my words and smiles!"

Get an accountability partner: An accountability partner is like your coach or mentor, colleague or even your spouse, but must be someone you hold in high esteem. He helps to keep you in check and watch you stick to discipline. He or she often makes you feel uneasy until you get done the things you ought to do; things you have resolved to do within a stipulated time frame. The partner reminds you of what you are trying to develop as regards building your confidence level and ensures you keep practicing. To develop unmatched confidence, you need an accountability partner who can walk the path with you. Do you have an accountability partner? If none, get one today!

Develop positive emotions: In his book "Seat of the Soul," Gary Zukacs says that positive emotions empower and negative emotions disempower. Positive emotions of happiness, excitement, love and enthusiasm make you feel more powerful and confident. Negative emotions of anger, blame or hurt weaken you and make you hostile, irritable and unpleasant to be around. Remember, "An action repeated often becomes a cultured habit"—Anonymous.

Practise! Practise! Practise! And Practise! Intentionally and consistently, repeat all you've identified to work for you fearlessly on a daily until it becomes a habit. This is the easiest way to develop confidence that endears you to people, making them get to know you, like you, and trust your abilities or capabilities. This is also the surest way to sustain your journey of becoming phenomenal.

To culture the habit of developing unmatched confidence, brand it till you become it! In the words of Facebook Chief Operating Officer, Sheryl Sandberg, "We hold ourselves back in ways both big and small, by lacking self-confidence, by not raising our hands and by pulling back when we should be leaning in." Always remember, you are braver than you believe, you are stronger than you seem, you are smarter than you think, and twice as valuable as you ever imagined.

CONGRATULATIONS ON TAKING A STEP CLOSER TO BECOMING A PHENOMENAL. AFTER CONFIDENCE, WHAT'S NEXT?

ACKNOWLEDGEMENT

The journey to becoming has been surreal. The experiences and daily encounters that are life changing, has molded and still forming the process of my journey.

I am grateful that I can share from my experiences to help many young women walk and work towards the path of life's purpose, in clarity and confidence in other to enhance their potentials for improvement and global relevance.

I thank my beloved parents, late Richard and late Caroline (Nwanyikaibeya) and my lovely siblings: Adaudo, Akwa Onyeoma, Akuchi, Uchegold and Ugofavour, whose constant prayers, love and support serve as a motivation to keep pursuing my goals. I love you all so much.

I could not have completed this book without the help and support of my friend, editor, and publisher. Thank you Cornelius for painstakingly proofreading this book and for providing expert advice throughout the process. Thank you, for accepting to write the foreword, too. I am grateful for your support over the last decade.

Thank you, Gamechanger Media for helping to create beautiful designs for the book. I am grateful to everyone who supported me on this journey.

Finally, I thank God for Grace, Comfort, Strength, Wisdom, and resources to start and finish this book. Truly, I can do all things through Christ who strengthens me!

BOOK REVIEW AND FEEDBACK

Write to Chigaemezu Regina:

olua.regina@gmail.com

WhatsApp chat: **+234 806 561 6632**

Join her Mentorship Community on Facebook: **Capacity Building Network**